Making Costumes for School Plays

Making Costumes for School Plays

JOAN PETERS AND ANNA SUTCLIFFE

Publishers PLAYS, INC. *Boston*

First American edition published by Plays, Inc. 1971

Library of Congress Catalog Card Number: 72–107967
ISBN: 0–8238–0083–0

© *Joan Peters and Anna Sutcliffe 1971*

Filmset in 11 on 12 point Monophoto Apollo
by Filmtype Services Ltd, Scarborough, England
Printed and bound in Denmark by F E Bording Limited
for the Publishers Plays, Inc., Boston, Mass. 02116

Contents

Acknowledgment

The authors would like to thank the following for their help and encouragement: The Chief Education Officer of Leeds; Miss J. Harland, Principal of the James Graham College, Leeds; Mrs A. Sugden, Headmistress of West Park County Secondary School for Girls, Leeds; the staff and students of the James Graham College, especially the students in the Main and Subsidiary Art and Main English Courses, and the pupils of West Park School. Also Malcolm Sunderland, Terence Shannon and Anne Mosedale for their great practical help during the preparation of the book.

Acknowledgment and thanks are also due to Edward Grinham and his students for taking the majority of the photographs, and to Philip Clemishaw for figures 20, 100, 111 and colour plate 3; Howard Fountain for figure 33 and colour plate 4; Alan Gummerson for figures 1, 39 and 103; John Henstock for figures 4, 121, 122 and 128 and the Yorkshire Evening Post for figures 19, 101 and 119.

Introduction

To those who are committed to the use of drama, and related activities in education, it comes as a surprise that the excitement of creating in form and colour in costume, as well as through words, movement, lighting and scenery should so often be ignored.

Costumes are sometimes regarded simply as a chore, to be given to the overburdened needlecraft department in a girls' school, and in a boys' school, what on earth is to be done unless the costumes are hired!

We do not underestimate the value of expert cutting and craftsmanship in the making of costumes. Many books exist on the history of costume and on cutting and sewing, including the correct patterns of period costume. We refer those who are interested in this work, to the many excellent books mentioned in the bibliography. But we are concerned here rather to extend the scope of the work and to show how a very wide range of creative activity and improvisation can contribute to the school play costumes, giving opportunities for imaginative work to many more children. For those of our readers who are daunted by their lack of expertise in cutting and sewing, we offer various suggestions for very simple methods of construction. We are not at all in favour of fashionable gimmicks: we believe strongly in the need to evoke the characteristic style of a period, but we also believe that the stage performance is an illusion, and that the mere slavish copying of the details of a period is not the most important thing. Costume design in school is not necessarily comparable to that in the theatre where the work of a creative designer will be faithfully interpreted, and the actual task of making will afford little or no individual opportunity for the maker. In school there must be scope for the individual to contribute, and this is one reason why we suggest that costume plays (all things being equal) sometimes have the greatest educational value.

We are aware that much thinking is going on about the place of drama in the curriculum, and its relation to other areas of study. We have every sympathy with the efforts being made to develop the awareness of children through improvisation, mime and regular work in the classroom, but we are convinced that the production of plays, and/or works involving music and dance, as complete works of art involving many creative contributions, should not be abandoned.

School productions can be a drain on time, and on everybody's energy, but they must surely be regarded as serious occasions for learning. To acquaint young people with important texts and to help the understanding of these by visual means is as urgent as anything we can undertake. We personally have not always had good texts with which to work, but we would not encourage the production of unworthy material. If a school, or school group production is to be worth while, we would suggest that teachers of English, as indeed many do, consider the visual possibilities of their choices, at least some of the time, and that more art teachers might come to regard theatrical design as being of comparable importance with painting or sculpture.

Materials

REMEMBER, NEVER THROW ANYTHING AWAY!
Some useful items for collection
Old sheets, blankets, curtains, bedspreads
Old evening and cocktail dresses (often found at jumble sales)
Tray cloths, lace table cloths, all kinds of braid, and crochet edging
Lace, ribbon, fringing, frills, seams and edging
Old and broken costume jewelry, beads, feathers, broken mirror, coloured glass
Lead foil from wine bottle tops, any small metal articles (screws, nuts, paper clips) tin lids, beer bottle tops
Plastic articles, particularly polythene lids, various cartons, bottle stoppers
Scraps of fur and leather
Shoes and high boots
Felt and straw hats
Sacks and sacking
Shirts, especially white or plain colours
Jumpers and cardigans, socks (three quarter white ones are especially useful for eighteenth century plays), heavy tights, thick coloured stockings, old trousers of all kinds

Suggested new materials
In addition to cheap, unbleached calico, or other cheap fabric, you may need new material. If so, furnishing remnants, often half price, are much the best buy, being usually wider and heavier than dress fabric at the same price. Take care however, because some of the thinner modern rayons hang and light badly, and are difficult to use for period costumes. When buying wool, sale bargains in dress and coat fabrics are sometimes available, and tubular jersey wool is a good investment. Nothing surpasses wool.

The work illustrated in this book is printed with *Helizarin* or printer's ink but any pigment printing process such as *Tinolite/Printex*, *Polyprint*, *Bedafin*, etc. may be used. All dyeing is done with *Dylon*, *Procion* or cheap aniline dyes, although any other home dyes are suitable.

1   *Jane and the 'bit box'*

2   ABOVE *Feathers, metal waste, beads*

3   BELOW *Feathers, seed pods and other useful items*

Notes on style

It is important to bear in mind that all parts of a production must ideally make up a satisfying whole. A usual practice in the theatre is to have very rich costumes and properties in a very simple set. Sometimes there is no actual set at all, the backstage area being revealed, and the costumes made up during the action, from items in a hamper—a typical 'alienation effect'. Sometimes the set will be an abstract arrangement of ramps, rostra, etc with no attempt to depict an actual place. What is necessary is that the set should be constructed to help the movement and action. However, these practices should not be taken as an excuse for making set and costume that contradict one another. We once saw an exquisite set made entirely in paper sculpture, but it did not work against spun-rayon dresses. If authentic costumes are used (and quite a lot of genuine Victorian costumes may be available), remember that these were made for close scrutiny, and if all the costumes are made in the same idiom to suit them, the result may be too refined for the stage. It may be better to make everything, however desirable great-granny's cape may be. These things *can* be used and often are—we have used many original articles, especially feather boas, gloves, hats and parasols: but be aware of the problems. Sometimes children, dancing class pupils especially, have access to very well-made professionally cut historical costumes. It is often heartbreaking not to use such articles, but they should be used only if the work in school can be done in the same idiom, and with the same kind of expertise. This may well be easy for the needlecraft department, but it may inhibit other kinds of creative work.

Some parents are often most anxious to help the school, and may be prepared to rig out their children at considerable expense, but this help must be declined if the rest of the production is likely to fail to reach this standard of cut and fabric. It may be frustrating for Titania if she is firmly told that she cannot wear her tutu (the most expensive one in the ballet group at that), but it is going to be necessary if the rest of the play is in Greek costume!

Some schools, we gather, convinced that they cannot organise the work themselves, and without the money to hire costumes, simply leave each cast member to contrive a costume with the help of parents. Much fun may result, but getting any unity is difficult. In our experience, the golden rules are: start early, plan ahead, work steadily towards the goal; or improvise at the last moment with dash and simplicity. Do not rely on the school down the road; and always have a great deal of raw material about. In most cases the 'rawer' the better.

Things we would deprecate: fruit-gum jewels, baking foil, cotton wool, milk bottle tops, crêpe paper and sometimes butter-muslin.

Many schools we know do devoted work and achieve miracles. It is not always the most polished results that indicate creative thinking, but those where an inspired translation of the available material is made.

It may be thought that many of our suggestions are no more than common sense, but often for one reason or another, the departments involved rarely coordinate, and it is to help make this happen that we have planned this book.

4 Making up in the art room, before an evening of dance/drama in which costumes of many periods were required. Being made up is a Charleston girl, the dress is authentic. The queue includes mediaeval lords and ladies. In the foreground is a Victorian maid wearing an authentic top (showing clearly the small size of many nineteenth century dresses), and a boy's woodwork apron with frills added. The Victorian cook on the right is similarly dressed

Basic fabrics—decorated and plain

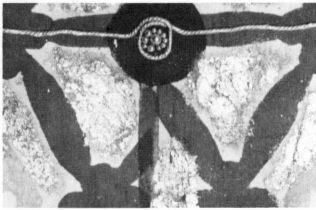

5   ABOVE *Appliqué on furnishing fabric, using scraps of various fabrics, some gold and some transparent. Also sequins, beads, plastic flower petals, etc., all freely stitched down by hand*

6   BELOW *Screen print, with additional potato printing, on dyed unbleached calico, with gold paint (powder in* Marvin Medium*), string and beads added*

For really good heavy draped effects, there is nothing better than old blanket. This is indeed preferable to compromising with inferior, cheap new material. This blanket brilliantly dyed, often tie-dyed or simply crumpled into the dye so as to take the colour unevenly, can give a splendid effect under stage lighting.

By far the best stand-by is old sheet and it is amazing how many of these are forthcoming when the need arises. Nothing takes dye better than old twill, especially when it is tie-dyed or blot dyed with brilliant and quite cheap aniline dyes such as those stocked by theatrical suppliers. If permanence to light and washing is essential then ordinary home dyes such as *Dylon*, *Drummer*, etc. may be used, or *Procion* or other re-active dyes. For the most part however school plays have short runs, and aniline dyes are cheaper and easier to use.

Heavy skirts may be made most effectively from old curtains, repp, brocade, faded velvet (this sometimes produces beautiful colours that light better than new, flat effects). Many furnishing brocades already have suitable patterns for Tudor and Renaissance costumes. If these form the basis of the design, they can be made more effective by the addition of beads and gilded cord.

To obtain texture and fresh colour on old, or cheap, plain fabrics the following materials and equipment are needed:
Polyvinyl acetate *(Marvin Medium)*
White emulsion pigment printing paste *(Helizarin Binder D (UK)*, *Alizarin (USA)*, *Tinolite Binder CM*, sold to schools and colleges in small quantities under the name *Printex (UK)*, *Versatex (USA))*
Rubber solution
Gold, bronze or nickel-silver powder
Lino or paint rollers
25 mm or 50 mm (1 in. or 2 in.) brushes
Powder paint
Printer's ink

14

Turpentine substitute

Pigment dyes (*Helizarin* (UK), *Alizarin* (USA), *Acco-Lite* (USA), or *Printex (Tinolite)*, *Versatex* (USA)).

For making a collage texture on the fabric, collect flower petals, fallen leaves, wood shavings, sawdust, fine sand, ferns, grasses, fabric shapes and scraps, beads, buttons, etc. Never throw anything away, old dyed string from tie-dyed fabrics is useful.

These may be glued at random, or in pre-arranged patterns on to the basic fabric until a rich crusty texture is obtained. The work can then be rolled flat, gold or other metallic paint and powder applied, and rolled again. This results in a varied rich texture which can be further enhanced with beads and jewels (sewn or glued), simulating the texture of fabrics featured in paintings by Rembrandt or Velasquez, rather than a slavish copy of actual textiles of the period. The slightly broken surface and contrast of light, especially if both gold and silver are used, can be most effective.

Of course if metallic fabrics are not desired, the materials can be used alone, and dye painted when the glue is dry.

If a very soft draping effect is required, we suggest painting the basic fabric with a pigment binder and metallic powder, rather than using *Marvin Medium* which will stiffen the fabric, if the pieces are then sewn by hand or machine, the result will drape well. Sewing by machine through gilded fabric is difficult, so where possible leave ungilded edges. It is impossible to machine-sew through fabric treated with *Marvin Medium*.

Yet another method of decoration, is the use of wax resist (batik), either alone or on top of existing appliqué or collage, or with collage and embroidery added (for details of batik techniques, see list of suggested books).

A good way of reproducing a pattern is to stencil melted wax through a template, subsequently cold-water dyeing the fabric. Free random painting of wax with a big brush, or drawing with a wax trailer are effective too.

Dripping paint or a mixture of paint and *Marvin Medium*, and perhaps metal powder, down the surface may be striking, alone or combined with collage and appliqué.

7 ABOVE *Gold powder in* Marvin Medium *thickly applied to old cotton jersey vest, pulled, stretched, sewn, flaked, with appliqué of beads and small metal objects. Intended to simulate worn, decorated gold leather*

8 BELOW *Old cotton net curtain painted gold, silver and bronze (powder in* Helizarin Binder D*), torn and cut fabric pieces (also metalised) all appliquéd on a background of black mull, daubed with gold and silver. The original mull which was left over from a previous costume, contained some machine embroidery, the whole making a rich but soft and easily draped fabric*

15

Screen printing, as well as painting dye through a stencil template may be used as a means of reproducing a design on fabric, this being subsequently decorated in any of the ways suggested. String collage or couching, though sometimes time-consuming, can be very attractive.

The reader will be able to think of many other interesting ways of decorating fabric. We give here the ones we have tried and found successful. Besides producing effective costumes, the creative work done on these fabrics may lead to many interesting developments in the art and craft rooms.

If paintings are used as inspiration, Venetian paintings, and the work of Rembrandt, Velasquez and Goya in particular are very helpful in inspiring textured effects, this close scrutiny will make children more familiar with the pictures. For another rich source of ideas see pictures of ancient artefacts—many are available now in colour magazines and paper backs. The rich effect of gold and jewelled objects found in tombs may very successfully be realised in a costume, as well as in actual jewelry.

9   Basic fabric of girl's dress, soft unbleached calico with poured and daubed gold and silver paint (metallic powder in Helizarin Binder D and Marvin Medium). Overskirt in rayon jersey. Boy's garment of dyed, heavy unbleached calico, with collage of braid, metalised scraps of needlecord, string, beads, etc. Yoke made from furnishing brocade, and hat of velvet and satin

10   Houpelande of blot dyed old bedspread, richly hand appliquéd with fabric scraps, beads, jewels, etc. Lining of sleeves made from faded velvet curtain. Hat from off-cuts of same bedspread. Fur collar from our collection

17

11 Three Kings. *Wearing from left to right: old sheet tie-dyed in three colours with gold fabric collage added. Chain of gold painted scrap materials and beads. Hat from dyed sheet wound round the crown of an old hat. The second King in tie-dyed costume with added decoration. Hat made from old curtain fabric. Heavy collar made from tufted carpet with applied beads and other metal objects, all painted gold. The third King's costume was cut from a pattern in a book on historic costume, and made from dyed curtains. Collar made from gilded fabric with appliqué of string, beads, etc. Gold, Frankincense and Myrrh are shown in greater detail on page 73*

12   Panel of stiff fabric made as follows: old curtain
fabric thickly layered with dead leaves (not too brittle),
straw, beads, etc. Glued with **Marvin Medium**. A varied
metallic surface was obtained by rolling over the panel
using a rubber linoleum block roller covered with gold,
bronze and silver powder in **Marvin Medium**. The natural
colour of the leaves occasionally shows through, and adds
yet another effect. The whole simulates quite effectively, a
certain kind of heavily embroidered fabric shown in
Renaissance portraits. Overskirt of very cheap, blot dyed
rayon taffetta

19

13 Sleeveless coat over Elizabethan dress. Made from half price furnishing repp painted with gold powder in Helizarin Binder D. *Inside faced with brocade remnants. Collage of embroidery from an old dress, hydrangea florets, fabric scraps, many old brooches and other small items of jewelry (in some cases simply pinned on), beads and sequins. This fabric is all gold, but the black of the embroidery and the various colours of some of the jewelry show through and add variety*

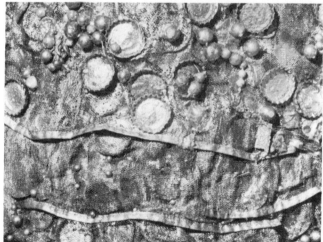

14   Close-up of back of coat, showing application of flower petals

15   ABOVE Close up of front, showing embroidery taken from old evening dress

16   BELOW Close-up of detail in the girl's costume shown in colour plate 2 (facing page 65). This shows clearly the method of layering net, dripping gold, and collage

felt strips, buttons, fabric scraps, lace, beads, etc. Three shades of gold powder in Helizarin Binder D have been used, with black ink painted into some of the cracks to enhance the shadow effect. The set-in sleeves are made from tarlatan and old coat lining. The head ornament is an old metal belt sprayed bronze

18   RIGHT *Doublet made from rayon furnishing fabric with heavy appliqué of fabric scraps, beads, etc., including piped velvet. Chain made from heavy cord with old buttons. Ruff made from organdie sewn with pearls. Semi-circular cloak uses scraps of velvet in panels, with satin bands freely embroidered by hand and machine. The fabric pieces are fixed down by sewing machine, ignoring raw edges which add vitality when lit. The cloak is lined with furnishing repp. This whole garment is extremely rich and heavy, illustrating the value of time and effort spent in enrichment rather than relying on the immediate effect of limp new fabric*

17   LEFT *Early nineteenth century dress in white rayon jersey. The skirt has been added to the top of an existing dress which has been gilded and heavily worked with string,*

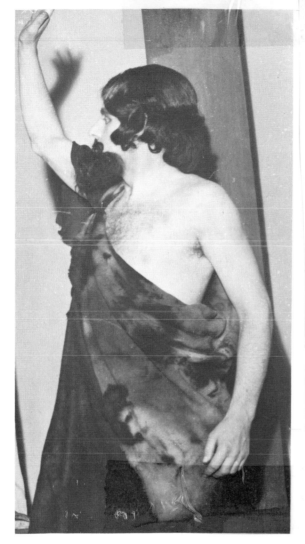

19 LEFT *Ragged nomad dressed in improvised costume—a piece of old blanket, showing the useful result of blot dyed fabric. The blanket was immersed in black aniline dye, which was in a small container, preventing even dyeing. We had no real control over the result, but we felt that it gave a good representation of the effect of mould on fabric*

20 RIGHT *Greek costume, easily made from blot dyed sheets. For the full effect of this technique see colour plate 3 (facing page 80)*

21 *Semi circular cloak in dyed blue satin cotton, with very simple raw-edge appliqué shapes fixed on by sewing machine, in dark green and scarlet. This cloak, used in a production of* Tiger At The Gates *was one of several stressing bold and simple pattern in combination with highly textured dresses and dull blot dyed rags*

22 *Sample of heavy decoration of fabric, using tin lids, peacock feathers, large beads, charred polythene, and the whole sprayed gold. The backing is of heavy hessian, unevenly dyed. This is an example of a heavy luminous treatment which may be suitable for hangings, tabards, cloaks, armour, etc*

Panels—decorated skirts, bodices and cloaks

For people who love creative work in collage, printing, simple or complex stitchery, appliqué, hand or machine embroidery, one of the most satisfying ploys may be the making of dress panels. These, both for skirts and bodices, are particularly suitable for Renaissance plays, and especially for court characters—so Shakespeare, Beaumont and Fletcher, or Marlowe, may give many a happy hour to children who would otherwise be far from the centre of things, because of their lack of interest or ability in acting or dressmaking.

We have illustrated various ways of making these. The most appealing thing is that any and every scrap may be used—fabrics, beads, trimmings, seams, junk, string, felt scraps, etc. The effect may be carefully drawn out first and worked symmetrically, as these designs would indeed have been, or it may be a free-textured creation, aiming at an impressionistic effect. All the methods described in the chapter on the decoration of fabrics may be used, except that sometimes the panels may require the greatest detail, definition and richness because they are the focus of the costume.

If you are lucky enough to have velvet or heavy brocade for the basis of the dress, it may require no other ornament, the detail can then be supplied by sleeves, yokes and front panels, and even by cloaks and redingotes.

A dress in humbler material may need decoration all over to bring it to an equal point of glory, but the two may be combined. *The Winter's Tale* or *Love's Labour's Lost* lend themselves especially to rich decoration of this kind, and if these dresses are mixed judiciously with an occasional foil in black, or a single bright colour, the result may be very satisfying. Alternatively the richness may be the one splendid thing in a group of drab ones, and thus achieve some sort or revelatory quality.

We have made a rich ecclesiastical costume for Becket in *Murder in the Cathedral,* which stood out against priests, monks and women, thus making the character—we hoped —seem as if decked out for sacrifice.

23 Becket from Murder in the Cathedral. *Chasuble made from the skirt of an old summer dress with a convenient check pattern. This was decorated with gold brush work (powder in* Helizarin Binder D) *and sewn with gold painted cotton net, the garment lined with cheap red taffetta. The stole is made from felt with successive layers of felt stapled on. Many colours of felt were used, and some of these show slightly through the gold and silver paint. This item is finished with gold cord, pearl beads and theatrical jewels. The alb is cheap white cotton, trimmed with white cotton net curtain and old braid. The mitre by the same method as the stole*

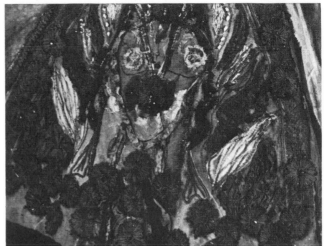

24   Cloak made from old furnishing brocade, with velvet, taffetta and beads added. About six colours were used in the garment, which produces a vitality when freely organised, an effect not always achieved by slavish copying of originals

25   ABOVE *Back of cloak. A subtle range of black, green and bronze, with very free machine stitching with a swing needle machine. The circles at the hem of the cloak were retrieved from an old Victorian cloak which was beyond repair. The garment is finished with hanging beads*

26   BELOW *Semi-circular cloak made from blot dyed curtain, decorated with very bold collage glued onto the cloak (almost no sewing), using velvet, cotton net and soft cord, in a range of reds and oranges, all produced by dyeing. Be careful when using collage this way, not to spoil the hang of the garment by using too much glue*

27

27   Costume made from a velvet furnishing remnant. The panel and undersleeves are old satin, and the design entirely collage, with sewn beads added. The ruff and partlet are of organdie

28   Front panel worked on dress satin, using gilded string
and cord, beads, old buckles etc. The overskirt is made from
an old yellow cotton brocade curtain covered with nylon
dress net, which had been previously gilded. (When gilding
dress net be sure to rest it on plain fabric; the gold dripping
through the holes will decorate the backing fabric, which can
then be used for something else.) The net was fixed to the
curtain fabric by free machine stitching in dark red which
added a little life to the overall dull gold effect. The pattern
round the edge of the overskirt was made by cutting out
pieces from the daubed black mull which is illustrated in the
chapter on decorated fabrics. The entire skirt was heavily
sewn with beads. This dress illustrates the vitality that can
still be obtained when using a monochrome range of rather
soft colour, simply by varying the tones and textures

29 LEFT *Dress based on shape often seen in German paintings (though panel is not typical). This garment, apart from the rich trimmings of panel and sleeves, is made entirely of blot dyed old sheets, mainly in sky blue and geranium pink. Given time spent on decoration, costume of this period does not necessarily demand rich fabric*

30 RIGHT *Close up of panel showing work in progress. This shows clearly the use of free brush work and net appliqué very freely applied (beads and jewels to be added)*

31 LEFT *Two Italian Renaissance costumes. Woman's dress is made from bridal brocade bought in a sale, and machine embroidered with net, gold cord and beads. This is a rich and comparatively expensive garment, but given time, money and expertise, not beyond the resources of a school. Although a straight stitch machine was used, and the design freely drawn, a similar design could be produced by swing needle, and the design drawn with the aid of a template or embroidery carbon. If machine embroidery is to be used, then it is essential that the panel be decorated before being attached to the dress. The man's costume was built onto a shape which was designed on the wearer in unbleached calico, and then covered with scraps of rich material, mainly black grosgrain and white velvet, sewn in stripes, afterwards carefully sewn with pearls and jewels. For details and close up of sleeves see illustrations 47 and 49. In contrast to some techniques we have shown, these costumes required the skill of good dressmakers*
32 RIGHT *Close up of panel showing peacock*

33　LEFT *Costume for Lady MacDuff, the main
construction in furnishing velvet, with richly embroidered
sleeves and panel using fabric scraps*
34　RIGHT *Close-up of front panel, very many different
fabric scraps and beads were used, fixed by machine and by
hand, also centres of net curtain flowers, crochet doylies, and
eyelet embroidery (cut from an old evening bag). This dress
is extremely rich and afforded maximum creative
experience for the designer. A very soft muted range of
colour was used, in order to conform to the needs of the
character and still have great richness*

35   Back fastening of Lady MacDuff's dress, showing
technique of concealing zip. Although zips are absolutely
essential for quick changes, they are disturbing to the
audience if visible

36   Close-up of bodice front, showing detail of embroidery,
the ruff is made of gold sprayed organdie. This in fact
turned out khaki—sprays are often of limited value, though
sometimes essential for last minute alterations. However,
this colour accident was very successful

33

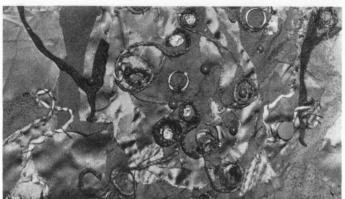

*worn by the man, is from pieces of velvet and lamé,
stitched onto a calico base, with braid and fabric scraps
freely applied by machine. The pants are based on a pair of
men's shorts covered with satin lining, with bands of
furnishing fabric*

38 **ABOVE RIGHT** *Close up of panel on scarlet dress satin,
decorated with fabric scraps in various shades of red, beads,
dyed string, buttons, curtain rings, etc. This fabric indicates
that an impressionistic effect of colour and texture involving
various degrees of luminosity, rather than a steady pattern,
may be effective*

39 **BELOW** *Top of a dress in scarlet velvet, showing
heavy appliqué based mainly on a string vest sprayed gold.
A large variety of beads and jewels give a rich effect*

37 **LEFT** *Venetian costume—the overskirt of the woman's
dress made from furnishing fabric in raspberry red, blot
dyed with orange. This device produced the kind of luminous
richness associated with Venetian painting. The doublet*

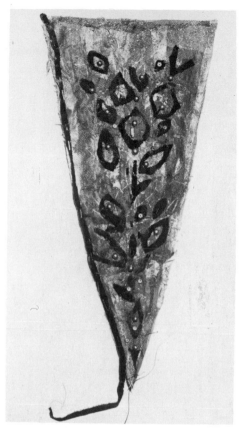

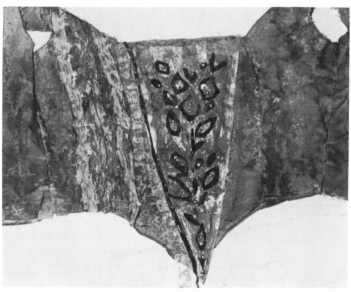

40   ABOVE LEFT *Bodice cut out and darted (made from a basic blouse pattern—to be found in nearly all pattern books). Made from cotton, blot dyed and stippled freely with a scrubbing brush dipped in various shades of green and blue. The left side shows strips of taffeta freely torn being fixed with pins for sewing*

41   ABOVE RIGHT *Pointed front panel showing free appliqué of net, beads, fabric scraps and broken chain, mounted on cotton and backed with heavy vilene. A stiff foundation is necessary for this part of the dress*

42   BELOW LEFT *Shows the panel mounted on the bodice, ready for making up and decorating*

43 and 44   Back and front views of a late Victorian dress made from very cheap unbleached calico, the bodice and overskirt made from voile. The bodice has been made from a simple blouse pattern and trimmed with beads, buttons, lace scraps, etc, to simulate a Victorian shape. The sleeves are period lace from an old garment. Many of the frills and flounces are made from old tablecloth edging, etc. This costume indicates the possibilities of combining old and authentic, with modern and synthetic, without conflict

45   Seventeenth century costume made from old fabric. No yardage was available, and this was made from the random contents of the bit box. Namely, an old loose chair cover, Terylene curtains, many pieces of lining taffeta, beads, ribbon, etc

Sleeves

One good practice we have found is to make sleeves, where appropriate, a very important feature of a costume. If these sleeves are made detachable—as was indeed the case in certain periods, especially during the Renaissance, it is possible to alter costumes from time to time, with little trouble. Sleeves from the fifteenth to the seventeenth centuries, and occasionally beyond these dates, can be composed of many tiers and layers of different materials, fixed either onto an existing garment with straight sleeves (old bodice ·or cardigan), or mounted on straight sleeves made from very cheap material. This not only uses up scraps, it creates a lively effect from the play of colours and different textures. The scraps can of course be dyed, and 'blot' dyeing will add to the variety of colour and texture. Beads or bits of jewelry, or other sight catching objects can be sewn or glued on, and will add to the effectiveness of the sleeves when lit.

There are many ways of constructing sleeves, we give three suggestions in our diagrams. For those who wish to keep cutting and sewing to a minimum, old frilled curtain pelmets, or ruffled curtain tops can be decorated and used effectively to make elaborate sleeves. Another useful source of sleeve material is the top of flared or fully gathered skirts from evening or cocktail dresses, especially those made of grosgrain, satin, velvet, etc. These often crop up in jumble or rummage sales. One such skirt cut in half or four, will make a good basis for a full sleeve. An existing bodice will often form the basic top of a costume, using the skirt to make full sleeves. Old coat linings frayed slightly and faded to soft subtle colours are good to use for parts of sleeves, ruched and gathered, and combined with other bits, these often look better than newly-bought, rather brash and modern looking fabrics of the same sort.

It is often difficult to convince people that old material may really be preferable to new, but we suggest that they abandon their prejudice and try effects with lighting.

38

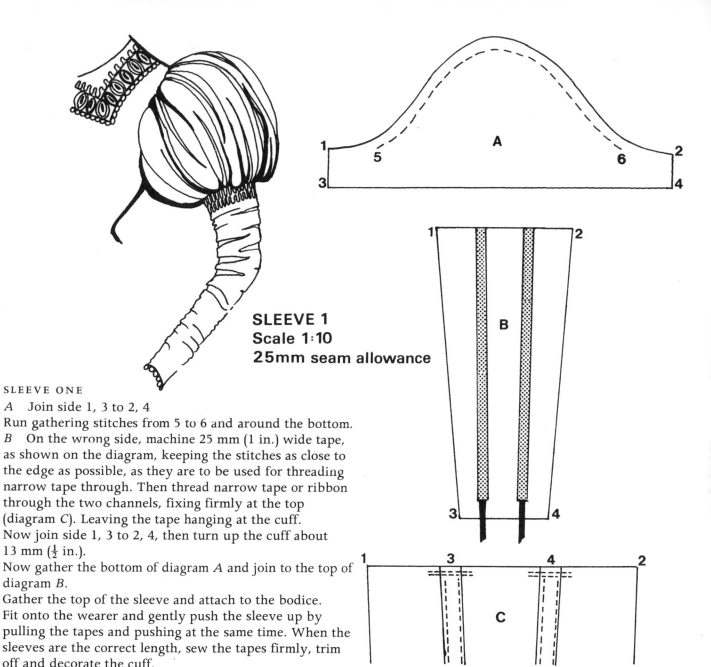

SLEEVE 1
Scale 1:10
25mm seam allowance

SLEEVE ONE

A Join side 1, 3 to 2, 4

Run gathering stitches from 5 to 6 and around the bottom.

B On the wrong side, machine 25 mm (1 in.) wide tape, as shown on the diagram, keeping the stitches as close to the edge as possible, as they are to be used for threading narrow tape through. Then thread narrow tape or ribbon through the two channels, fixing firmly at the top (diagram *C*). Leaving the tape hanging at the cuff.

Now join side 1, 3 to 2, 4, then turn up the cuff about 13 mm ($\frac{1}{2}$ in.).

Now gather the bottom of diagram *A* and join to the top of diagram *B*.

Gather the top of the sleeve and attach to the bodice.

Fit onto the wearer and gently push the sleeve up by pulling the tapes and pushing at the same time. When the sleeves are the correct length, sew the tapes firmly, trim off and decorate the cuff.

39

Much of the movement in a play is that of gesture and arm movement. If the actors know that their arms are well dressed, this will be an encouragement to use them more eloquently.

46   Variation of sleeve based on diagram 1, in brown grosgrain on Italian Renaissance dress

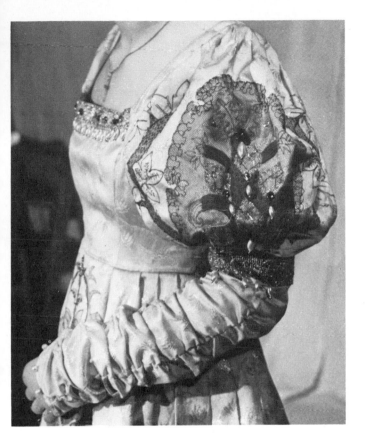

47   Sleeve based on diagram 1, heavy dress fabric (see illustration 31). Top of sleeve machine embroidered with appliqué on net, sewn with beads and jewels

48   Variation on diagram 1, blister nylon dress fabric in rich red, with freely applied strips in various red fabrics. This sleeve depends for effect on the play of light on textured surfaces, and variety of one colour. Note, the forearm is not ruched, but straight to the wrist

49   Man's doublet sleeve made from velvet and lamé,
scraps of rich fabric mounted on calico. Woman's dress as
previous illustration with ruff removed to provide Venetian
rather than Elizabethan effect

50   LEFT *Sleeve based on diagram 1, using a piece of frayed fabric (damaged factory reject). The puff is made of soft nylon, with strips of fabric in off-white shades, applied at random, and subsequently held by a layer of net, fixed by machine embroidery to provide stiffness*

51   RIGHT *Close up of original fabric showing decorative use of fraying. With practice, faults and accidents of this kind can be used creatively*

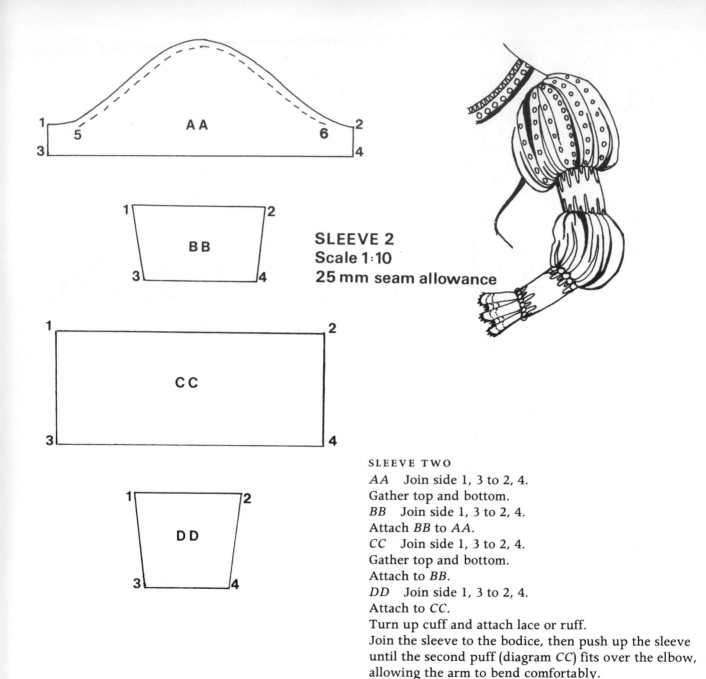

SLEEVE 2
Scale 1:10
25 mm seam allowance

SLEEVE TWO
AA   Join side 1, 3 to 2, 4.
Gather top and bottom.
BB   Join side 1, 3 to 2, 4.
Attach *BB* to *AA*.
CC   Join side 1, 3 to 2, 4.
Gather top and bottom.
Attach to *BB*.
DD   Join side 1, 3 to 2, 4.
Attach to *CC*.
Turn up cuff and attach lace or ruff.
Join the sleeve to the bodice, then push up the sleeve
until the second puff (diagram *CC*) fits over the elbow,
allowing the arm to bend comfortably.

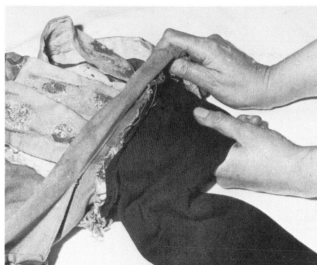

52   Sleeve of German style dress (see illustration 29) made
from many multi-coloured scraps of fabric, a variation of
diagram 2. This photograph shows felt scraps being stapled
onto sleeve bands

53   Same sleeve showing wool cardigan sleeve fitted inside
(see instructions for making up page 44)

SLEEVE 3
Scale 1:10
25mm seam allowance

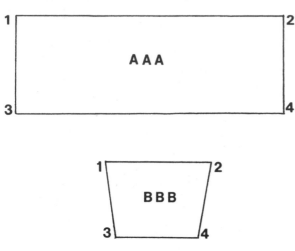

```
1                          2

        A A A

3                          4
```

```
1                2

      B B B

  3              4
```

```
1                          2

        C C C

3                          4
```

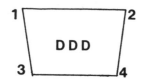

```
1              2

    D D D

  3            4
```

**Using diagram A
and top of
diagram B
from preceeding pages**

SLEEVE THREE

Use diagram *AA* from sleeve two.
Use the top 305 mm (12 in.) of block *B* from sleeve one, draw up to 178 mm (7 in.). Join this to the puff from sleeve two, and make up the rest of the sleeve as in two.

NB   These sleeves when finished are approximately 914 mm (36 in.) long, and must be adjusted to fit the individual. It is essential that the pieces between the puffs fit as tightly as possible. A simple way to keep the sleeves tight and puffed out, is the addition of an old woollen sleeve from a jumper or cardigan, which must be pushed through the sleeve before it is attached to the bodice, and then joined onto the bodice at the same time (see illustration 8). It is possible to add as many puffs as desired, by shortening the straights accordingly.

46

54   Sleeve based on diagram 3, very many different fabric scraps. In contrast to the previous sleeves, this one is worked and sewn meticulously (see Lady MacDuff illustration 33)

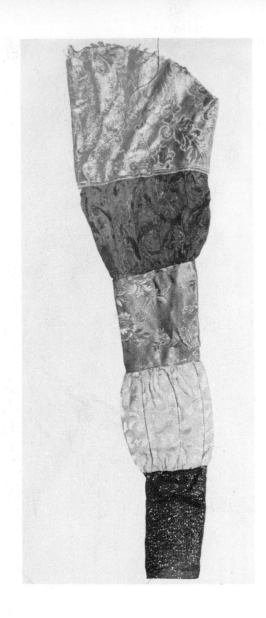

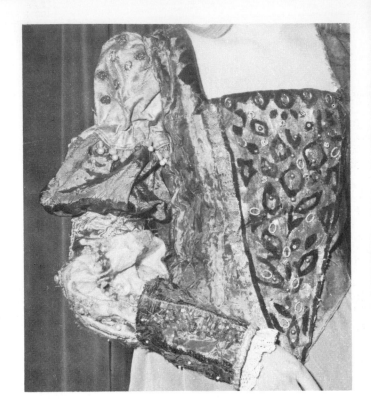

55 LEFT *Rudimentary stage of sleeve, made strictly according to diagram 2. Using any old brocade scraps, with lurex cuff*

56 RIGHT *Same sleeve showing decoration added. The harsh glitter of the cuff has been modified by means of torn strips of very old dress taffeta. Old fabrics of this kind, rotted beyond repair, though useless for major items, because of deterioration, can make a very valuable contribution to the softness and subtlety of period costumes which may offend if entirely constructed from modern synthetic fabrics. The full colour of this sleeve can be seen in plate 1 (facing page)*

PLATE 1 *Complete dress made up as follows: Sleeves made separately (see diagram on page 44 and figure 56). Bodice made separately (see figure 42). Skirt panel made separately, and mounted on a blot dyed sheet. The overskirt is made from a portion of an old blue velvet curtain, faded almost to grey in places. The panel and bodice are heavily beaded and jewelled, with the addition of much free appliqué work in various fabrics including nets of various colours. The whole dress includes numerous shapes of material all old, and no two pieces of colour exactly alike. The point we are stressing here is that a harmonious effect can be obtained this way, providing the colours are subtly blended. This is a range of blues, greens, greys and yellows. By these means a very satisfying effect may be achieved, which is sometimes preferable to new bright fabric which can be tedious to the eye. This technique encourages economy in materials and creative thinking*

57
grosgrain dau
old Dutch bli
cuff. This is s
required no p
materials

58   *Sleeve on a calico base, quite straight and very long, made from old curtain pelmets dyed dull brown and daubed silver, with original rufflette tape causing the double puff effect. Forearm, made from a piece of gilded bedspread, cuff made from gilded lace edged tray cloth*

59 Sleeve made from rayon brocade, originally silver and white, dyed emerald green. This sleeve is a simple shape, wide at the top, tapering to the cuff, and twice as long as the required arm length. Lack of decoration is compensated for by the play of light on deep ruching of very luminous fabric

60 Wide straight sleeve, with longer free strips fixed at cuff and gartered twice to give effect of double puff, requiring a minimum of sewing. This sleeve is in rich reds and oranges, and looks splendid under gold coat, see illustration 39

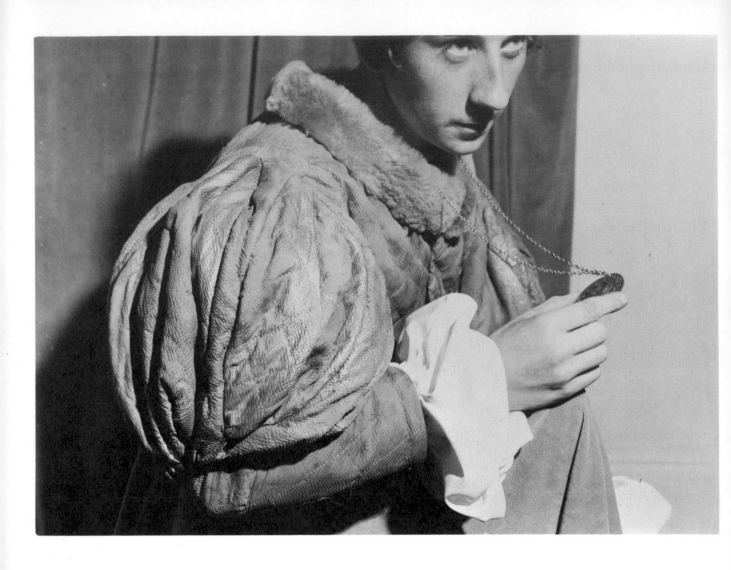

61 Doublet inspired by Titian painting, and made from a dyed quilted housecoat. Blue blot dyeing covers up original flower sprigs. The width of the puff has been achieved by slitting the original sleeves, and inserting strips cut from the skirt

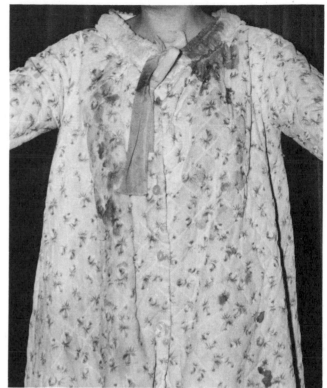

62 *Doublet in course of construction*

63 *Original dressing-gown, rejected when ruined by hair dye*

53

64 OPPOSITE LEFT *Sleeves with alternating puffs of old curtain fabric, picked out in gold and decorated with beads. This costume indicates once again, that yardage is not necessary in great quantity to make an effective costume, provided the dressmaker has patience and ingenuity*

65 OPPOSITE RIGHT *Long wide sleeve gathered at elbow with braid, and with deep tucks down the forearm. This sleeve was designed to use several scraps of rich material in the absence of full yardage*

66 ABOVE *Sleeve shown in illustration 64 being attached to doublet by means of eyelet holes*

67 *German doublet, using quilted coat lining with rich surface embroidery in red and white. The sleeves are dyed calico with felt scraps and padded decoration. The sword is made from filed aluminium, good for decoration, but not for heavy fighting*

68 *Shirt as worn under many tunics in this book. Very full white rayon jersey. This fabric is unbeatable for soft drape effects needing a certain amount of body*

Jewelry and headgear

Items to collect

Polythene lids, bottle tops, tin lids, cord and string, sealing wax, gold, silver and copper powder, *Marvin Medium*, black or sepia dye, paint or ink; chocolate and sweet containers; beads and costume jewelry, felt tabs, scraps of leather, thick cloth and hessian, clear glue, cheap chain, leather thonging, small metal articles of all kinds, old lino blocks, paint sprays, feathers of all kinds (including feather cuttings, feather dusters, layered feather hats), foam rubber, nylon and hair switches, milliners' canvas, wire and many other similar items.

Making stage jewelry can be a creative task for a whole group, or it can serve well as a spare time or interim activity, when a child finishes another piece of work early. It is easy to organise at home, needing little space. Though it may be desirable to have a certain unity in the work, scope can always be given for enterprising and imaginative use of materials, and for an individual's inspired improvisation.

It is important at the outset to study form. Eighteenth century girandoles will need different treatment from Celtic torques or Byzantine plaques. Nothing looks odder than glittering, many-faceted jewels on ancient Greeks. Facet cutting is a fairly late invention, and in many cases, a general impression of cabochon gems or garnet and glass, *cloisonné*, or wrought gold and slabs of lapis lazuli may be what is needed.

Here as with the fabrics, there is no need for slavish copying, as long as the general principles are borne in mind. The distance and lighting will produce half the illusion, and creative improvisation may be better than dogged imitation.

69   *Necklace of dyed* Marvin Medium *dried solid (the dye was dripped into the liquid medium before it began to solidify). Small beads were added, and the pieces strung together on fine thread*

70   *Bracelet made from scraps found in a work box, including paper-clips, hooks and eyes, necklace fastener, etc, plus broken Christmas baubles, and strands of pulled rubber solution*

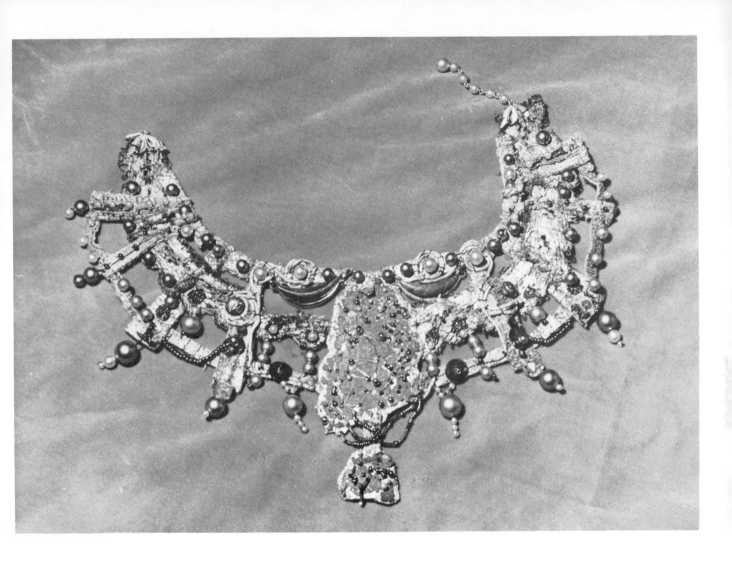

71   Collar with centre piece of corroded metal (found on
building site), the holes in the metal made it easy to sew onto
a piece of fabric, adding beads at the same time. The rest
made from felt and other stiff fabric, trimmed with buttons,
painted silver and sewn with pearls and small beads

59

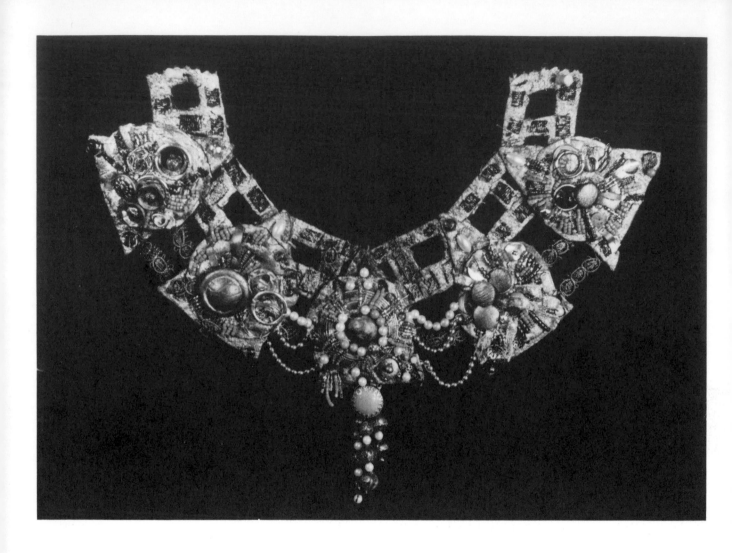

72   Collar made from old blanket and felt scraps, painted
various tones of gold, with buttons, beads, curtain rings,
string collage, and squares of blue lurex fabric (painted over
with ink). The full effect can be seen in the colour plate 2
(facing page 65)

73   Group of collars made by children as part of an art and
dance project, made from felt, blanket, buttons, beads, etc.
Bright colours on gold and silver painted fabric. Theme
Aztec

74 *Large collar, made on pleated linen, sewn with felt
strips and string collage, button trimmed, painted light and
dark gold. Beads and black ink added*

75 *Children working on mask and jewelry project*

76 *Pe*
buttons
Made in school for a Greek play

PLATE 2   *Group of children's costumes for an Easter play with a pagan theme. The individual items of jewelry appear in close-up in this chapter. Cloaks, loin cloths, etc, are simply draped and pinned, no sewing needed. Make-up simply achieved by applying cold cream to the skin and lightly dusted with the same powder we use for paint. This is very quick to do, and is easily removed with cream and tissues, followed by soap and water. The hair of the female figure had been built up with six nylon switches. The top part of her costume is made from an old cardigan painted liberally with gold powder in* Marvin Medium, *to imitate the top of a Sumerian costume, the tiered skirt made from cheap cotton fabric is very heavily covered by means of collage and appliqué with beads, string, net, buttons, fabric pieces and very many beer bottle tops. Gold paint has been dripped over the costume which when dry was immersed in black dye, and dripped and splashed with gilt once more. This is a very elaborate costume requiring much time, but any of the above effects may be used singly, giving an effective but less rich and complex costume if time is not available. A close-up of the skirt decoration can be seen in decorated fabrics, illustration 16. Time may sometimes be afforded for a costume of this kind if most of the other costumes are created with great simplicity. Designers should use their own judgment. The richness produced by texture in one costume can be balanced by the intensity of colour and luminosity in some of the others. For close-up and details of jewelry see illustrations 72, 74 and 79*

77 and 78 Two groups of items made for Norse Warriors. String, beer bottle tops, dressmaker's weights, metallic fabrics, beads, cardboard, various metal items, an old lino block, leather thonging, polythene lid, canvas, etc

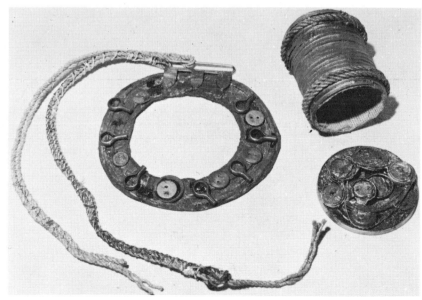

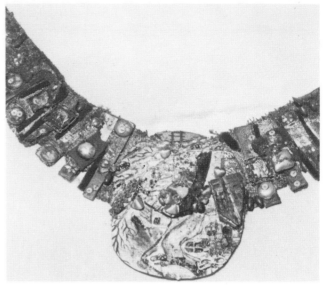

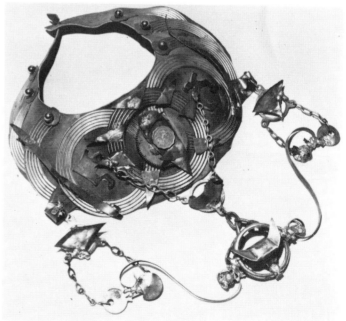

79   A B O V E L E F T *Collar based on gold painted fabric with small slabs of lino wired through. The lino is coloured with various metallic powders in* Marvin Medium. *Beads and fabric added (see also colour plate 2, facing page 65)*

80   A B O V E R I G H T *Collar on gold painted fabric. The main decoration is a lino block which had been previously used for print making in school, this has been painted gold, and beads, buttons, etc have been freely added. (Never throw old lino blocks away)*

81   B E L O W R I G H T *Collar based on old leather cut from a school satchel, soldered metal objects, including chains, keys, coins, etc, applied with* Marvin Medium

82   *Head-dress made with chicken wire and various kinds of swarf (metal turnings)*

83 and 84 (OPPOSITE) *Demonstration of head-dress built up from four black nylon switches, with bird pelt centre-piece (covering hairgrips and join), beads, various feathers. No preliminary work required. Ear-rings made from tassels from old feather boa attached to existing pair. Necklace from old beads and chains*

85 Helmet made from chicken wire, coarsely woven with great variety of torn fabrics (some metalised), with buckles, beads, etc. Tassels made from dyed unspun wool. Tunic of coarse fabric, with collage of dyed blanket, beads, cord, etc

86   *Crown on wire frame, fabric stiffened with* Marvin
Medium. *Decoration of wood-shavings, plastic prisms,
leather thonging, beads, buttons, broken glass, etc*

87   *Crown mounted on plastic band using items rejected
from other work, including broken combs, plastic building
kit pieces, small bottle brush, buttons, twigs and plastic
flowers*

71

88 *Head-dress made on a band previously used for stiffening a hat, decorated with feathers, plastic leaves, beads etc*

89 *Head-dress made on existing hat-band; feathers, beads and buttons*

90 ABOVE LEFT *Goblet made from cardboard carton with plastic leaves and flowers, shells, beads, etc painted gold*

91 ABOVE RIGHT Gold, Frankincense and Myrrh. *Made from a toffee tin and two wine bottles (extended with toilet-roll cores), decorated with beads, string, beer bottle tops, polythene lid, gold paint. All glued with* Marvin Medium. *(See illustration 11)*

92 CENTRE RIGHT *Cornucopia made from cardboard cone, extended with glued screwed paper, and finally layered with tissue paper. Decorated with pins, twigs, beads, wood shavings, dead leaves, etc*

93 BELOW RIGHT *Fan of assorted feathers. The centre is made from the bottom of a brass-wire fruit basket, and the handle from the rim of the same basket. Brooch pinned to centre. Held together with soft wire*

73

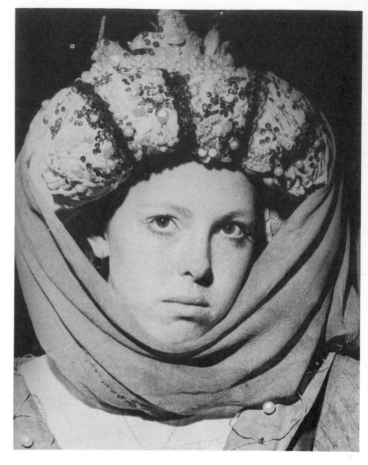

94   ABOVE LEFT *Crown made from the sides of the wire basket as used for the fan. Trimmed with diamanté, beads, wire, etc*

95   BELOW LEFT *Mediaeval head-dress made from wire and plastic foam, covered with painted millinery canvas. Decorated with sequins, beads and braid.*

96 (ABOVE RIGHT) *and* 97 (OPPOSITE LEFT)   *Mediaeval head-dresses made from millinery canvas, covered with fabric scraps, beads, etc, and chiffon drapes. The chiffon was bought very cheaply on a market stall*

98   ABOVE RIGHT *Crown made from wire covered with gold fabric, with beads and buckles added*

99   BELOW RIGHT *Bonnet made from the stiffening inside an old hat, as part of a test in creating headgear from old rubbish and throw away objects. This is painted gold and trimmed with beads and fabric*

cloth fabric, or knitted from string, and we feel that we
not enlarge on this, beyond saying once again that
r nickel powder in *Marvin Medium* or *Binder D*, may
e better and cheaper than the usual daubed or sprayed
er.

already mentioned, fantastic armour may be assembled
ly from all kinds of junk, using hessian, calico or
et as a base, in the form of a tunic, tabard or leotard.

A usual method of making plate armour is to soak felt in size, mould the shapes to the body and paint these. Felt yardage is however, very expensive, and old, closely-woven woollen cloth (blanket, old coats, etc.) may prove preferable.

100   Costume from The Bacchae, *calico tunic with sewn pieces of various metalised fabrics (gold, bronze and silver powder in* Marvin Medium, *with fabric colours showing through), mainly brown. On the surface, smaller pieces of gold painted fabric, old brooches, etc, glued with* Marvin Medium. *The edges of the garment bound with cord. The tunic lined with sheet wadding (old quilted dressing-gown will do), goes over a pleated cambric skirt. An attempt was made here to produce an impression of Greek armour, but to retain an abstract effect. The cloak is dark blue woollen jersey, edges left raw but neatened with pinking shears, as fabric hangs and drapes better with no hems and as few seams as possible. The sword was forged from an iron bar, and the hilt cast in bronze from a wooden pattern (not beyond the scope of a boys' metalwork department)*

101 OPPOSITE *Group of children wearing Greek costume in a wide variety of colours produced by blot dyeing old sheets. The armour in the foreground is a collage of various fabrics, mostly rich metallic effects, on old blanket.. The tunic skirts are strips of dyed sheet attached under the armour at the waist, and block printed with potato or lino. The printing, collage and the making of jewelry, for a cast of ninety children aged between eleven and sixteen, was made by children in art classes*

102 ABOVE *Detail of costume in illustration 101*

103 BELOW *Children working on armour and jewelry*

104　*Two girls wearing armour on basic tunics made from an old tablecloth. The tunics were decorated with collage in a wide variety of fabrics, including dyed blankets painted with size, cuttings of leather, sheet and blanket edges, and gold and silver painted scraps of fabric*

PLATE 3   *Photograph taken during a performance of*
The Bacchae *of Euripides, showing the effect of blot dyed,
simply draped old sheets, and very intense contrasting
colours against a sombre set. The shoulder drapes are
stencilled beige velvet, to simulate animal skins*

105 Four Greek costumes, using old sheets dyed orange,
pink and blue, with simple printing and added jewelry. The
armour tunic was originally made to fit a schoolgirl, this
kind of garment can easily be adjusted to fit most sizes, if a
generous wrap over is allowed at the back. The skirt can be
lengthened to suit the wearer

81

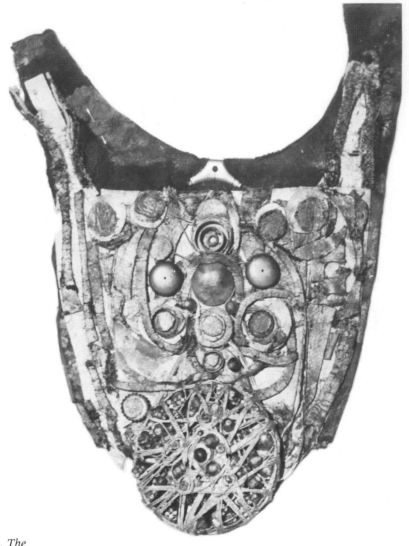

106　*Breast plate for Merlin from* Thor with Angels. *The basic fabric is a piece of reject batik heavily waxed and firm to sew. Metalised fabric, many metal objects, and a quantity of string have been applied with* Marvin Medium. *The boss was originally a round chocolate pack padded from the back to give weight and stability, and then decorated. The accidental green-bronze colour of the basic fabric, suited this character well*

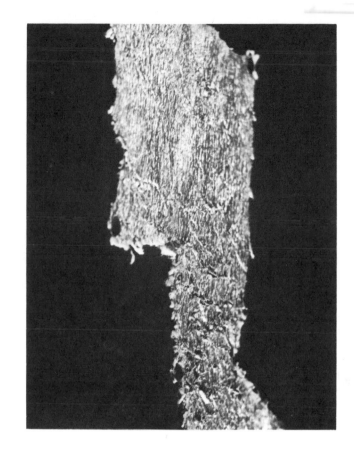

*107 and 108   Pieces torn from the inside of a wax lined
sack (for packing paraffin wax) and painted gold, this fabric
could be very useful for corroded armour and war gear*

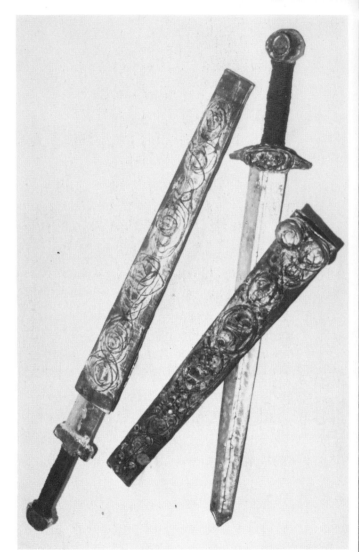

109 LEFT *Abstract shield made from squashed wire, coarsely woven with numerous fabrics and string, with decoration of broken glass*

110 RIGHT *Swords and scabbards, simply but heavily decorated with string and small metal objects. The blades are beaten tin over wood, and the scabbards are made of cardboard. We strongly advise that swords be metal or metal coated, not wood or plastic. Rapiers and broadswords may be made from filed aluminium, but they are not advised for practical fights as they buckle easily. If all else fails, hire the weapons*

84

111   Helmet made from chicken wire, layered with newspaper and Marvin Medium. *The crest is polystyrene, bound to a cardboard form with tissue paper and paste. Painted with* Marvin Medium *and gold powder (do not use a spray, this dissolves the polystyrene). The helmet is a silver gilt colour, with blue patches, unevenly daubed, to avoid a garish effect. The spear has a wooden shaft and a tin blade, dulled with black paint to make it look more substantial. The shield is cardboard, with a collage of torn net curtains coated in* Marvin Medium, *unevenly daubed with gold and silver. The cow device (representing Thebes) was built with cardboard shapes*

85

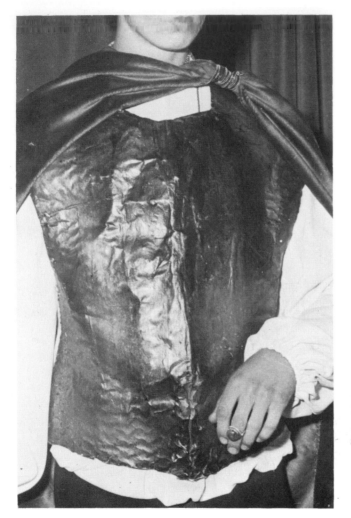

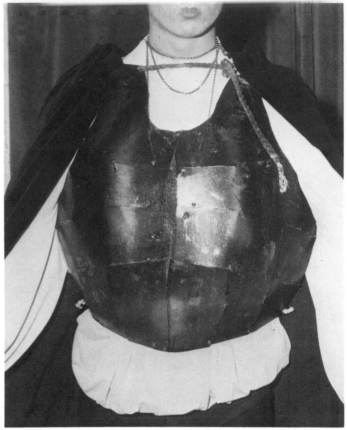

112 Breast plate made from chicken wire covered with
newspaper, sprayed black, green and gold for an
impressionistic metallic effect. This close-up shows detail of
making, but the effect when worn is intended to be blurred
by distance. This technique is not really suitable for any
performance involving close contact between actors and
audience

113 Metal breast plate, tin snipped to form darts and
bolted to form curves, made from white metal, sprayed
black, green and gold

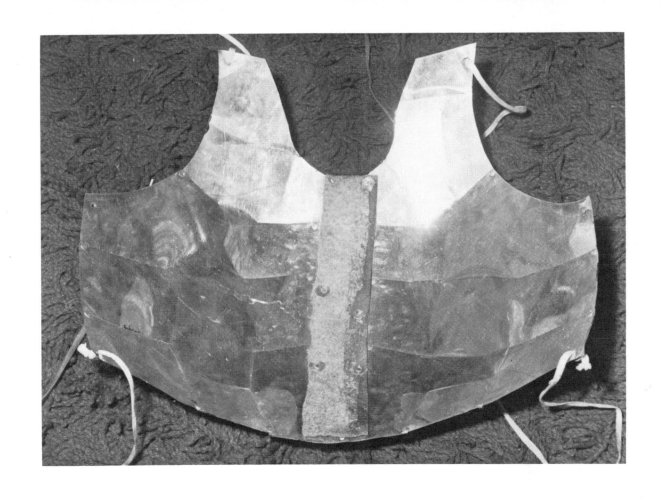

114 *Inside of metal breastplate showing fastenings and felt re-inforcements down centre*

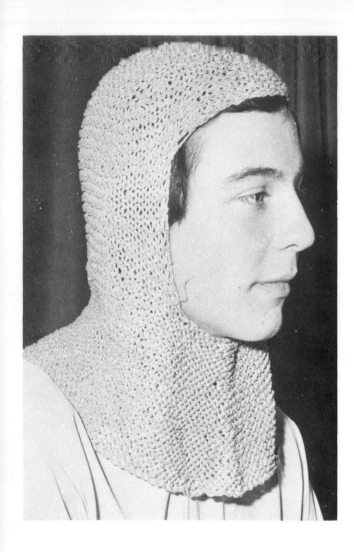

*115 Simple knitted helmet of string, painted silver with
powder in* Helizarin Binder D. Marvin Medium *may be
used, but this type of garment is better if flexible*

Peasant costumes

Clothing minor characters may be a very simple job, or it may be the most difficult and elaborate of all. Non-speaking lords and ladies often account for the greatest labour (and opportunity) in a costume play. St Joan, except for her armour, can be dressed in half an hour. A useful standard collection of oddments, for beginning the work of dressing peasants and the like, is as follows:

Old trousers

(trews, jeans, etc.) These can be cut down to form knee-breeches or long Elizabethan slops, or used short to act as a base for Elizabethan round hose—with the big advantage that they fit the characters with ease (especially if they have supplied their own garments). Be careful about fly-fastenings, it may be necessary to 'fake' flat fronts or cod-pieces.

Old socks

especially thick wool socks of plain dark colours (avoiding nylon), are invaluable for simulating soft shoes of all kinds. With length added to the toes they become mediaeval, with added laces and decoration, and with broad toe padding they do very well for tudor shoes, sprayed or painted with silver they do for mail shoes. Wear them over plimsolls for 'body'. Ordinary leather shoes on the whole, are too heavy for stage use, they tend to inhibit movement.

Old shirts

These with collars removed and 'pie frills' added for Tudor characters, or with bishop sleeves for Renaissance men.

Men's long underwear

(Long johns) These homely garments—sometimes cotton jersey, preferably wool—may sometimes be begged from neighbours and relatives, or bought fairly cheaply. Dyed, they make good tights, worn under hip-length tunics or doublets. They may be effectively cross-gartered, or simply

116 Sixteenth century ruffians, dressed quickly from odd items. Cut down trousers, dyed long underwear, socks over plimsolls, odd leather belts, worn shirts with frilled collars, old jumpers, tunics made from old blanket. All of these items were rapidly dyed in earth-coloured dye, which produced a variety of black, brown and green shades

worn with plimsolls under thick socks, rolled down. Modern stretch nylon tights tend to cling too closely, and are often too transparent. If tights are being bought, wool or cotton serve better, white cotton tights dyed are comparatively cheap. If only nylon tights are available, it is often a good idea to wear two pairs for thickness.

Thick woollen sweaters

These may be worn (having been previously dyed to 'blur' the surface and disguise the look of modernity) under tunics either sleeveless or wide sleeved, for either men or women.

When making costumes for female servants in Tudor plays, we have used sweaters with puffs added at the shoulders and ruffs or collars at the necks. If a tight fitting sweater is used the effect is quite adequate provided a fairly gathered skirt is worn over the jumper, and an apron tied over that. In such cases, the jumper-bodice should be stiffened, because a natural bosomy look is alien to Tudor style (study books of drawings and portraits). By omitting the puffs and ruffs, and fixing the skirt over the hip line, a more mediaeval effect may be obtained.

The universal old sheet may be pressed into service again for aprons, wimples or Tudor bonnets—a glance at a Dürer painting of humble women will give many ideas for twisting the fabric to make such caps, they simply need folding and pleating into shape over a headband, and pinning or sewing. Such articles may easily be blotched and dirtied, tattered and otherwise artistically deranged where suitable. It is sometimes a good idea to take the edge off glistening whiteness, especially where peasants are to be contrasted with court characters in white. Unbleached calico or twill is quite effective, as are old sacks for working aprons.

Sacks and blankets are the most useful articles for the making of tunics, either T-shaped or simple sleeveless bags, and for skirts. Often the more dirty and tatty the better—these items going on from year to year, getting more and more wretched, sometimes turn out to be the most effective and lightable of all. We advocate blot dyeing in shades of sepia, olive, and all kinds of dirty grey and black.

117　Group of peasants dressed in remnants of old sheets and curtains in colours taken from fresco paintings. These were the rude mechanicals in an Italianate production of A Midsummer Night's Dream

118 Mistress Quickly and serving wench, wearing blot dyed heavy furnishing fabric, hessian and old curtains, in a range of warm pinks and browns, with items of haberdashery in calico

119 (OPPOSITE LEFT) Serving man and woman from Macbeth, *wearing old shirts extended with bishop sleeves, with cuffs and pie frills added. The tunic made from oddments of fabric, dyed various browns. The woman is wearing cap made on the head, jumper with pie frills and cuffs added, skirt made from dyed bedspread, with calico apron. These garments were made rapidly from the very last remaining items, and they contrasted well in a range of rust, scarlet, green and mustard, with the richness of the principals' costumes*

Odd shapes of the same material, slung by means of a cord, serve well for cloaks, or they can be made to just fit the shoulders by gathering into a band that fastens across the chest.

Thick cord, old leather belts or dull looking chains can serve as fastenings. Monks are easily habited in this kind of gear, though they tend to require more yardage.

The drab, muted colours of these articles allow for endless re-combinations, fitting in with a wide variety of plays, and a brighter detail may be occasionally added, especially if a *Book of Hours* or Mediaeval manuscript is being used as inspiration.

Those playing murderers and other heavy character parts, usually delight in adding detail to sleazy detail of their costumes, and willingly black their teeth and tear their clothes, and hunt around for suitable knives, etc.

After every play, it is best to collect carefully as many humble items of this sort as possible—rough wooden crosses, cords, belts, carefully whittled daggers, leather wallets made from old stachels, rusty chains, patchwork bundles, shepherds crooks, plain steel knives, roughly trimmed staffs, broken stoneware crocks, and items of copper or pewter.

Basic peasants can be transformed into common soldiers by the addition of knitted mail items, leaving the work and materials available for noblemen's armour.

Greek, Roman and Near Eastern peasants need approximately the same treatment, with perhaps lighter weight material and occasionally sandals over bare feet. Modern sandals, however simple, seldom look right, especially if made of PVC or simulated leather. Cords twisted round the ankle from a simple sole, are better. Mediterranean sailors, naked to the waist and barefoot, may be characterised by the odd ear-ring and a bundle, with a knife in the folds of the loincloth. For this purpose, old ragged, coarse-woven tablecloths or bedspreads (especially striped) can be used, the older and thinner the material has worn, the better they drape.

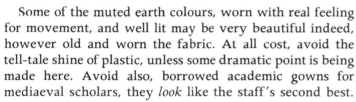

Some of the muted earth colours, worn with real feeling for movement, and well lit may be very beautiful indeed, however old and worn the fabric. At all cost, avoid the tell-tale shine of plastic, unless some dramatic point is being made here. Avoid also, borrowed academic gowns for mediaeval scholars, they *look* like the staff's second best.

Be careful about spectacles! If worn by mediaeval and later characters they should be round and nose-perched, Flemish painters are a marvellous source of ideas.

An effective group of revellers can be ruined if the serving girls are using an obvious plastic tray. Many ordinary items will serve for Greek and Roman goblets if they are painted, and decorations are added, but do look at the original sources, Greek vases are perhaps the most useful for this. All these details are obvious, but they are of paramount importance, and they really do make the difference between tattiness and quality.

120   Fifteenth century peasant, wearing a calico skirt attached to an old jumper. The stretching of the jumper has produced a long line, in contrast to the high waist of the court lady, since it might be supposed that the peasant fashions lagged behind. Though simple, this dress in yellow, green and pink worked well with the court dresses. In this play, The Lark, we dyed all the peasant linen slightly yellow to contrast with the pure white garments of the Dominican monks. Wimples of this sort need not be made-up beforehand, but can be rapidly improvised on the night

121 *Group of children dressed in old sheets and remnants,
in earth colours, worn over jumpers, tights and socks*

122   Costume for a dance, old blanket over a jumper.
'Norse' jewelry can be seen in close up in the chapter dealing
with jewelry

123   A page wearing an old shirt extended with rayon
jersey left over from regal items. The cloak is old,
undecorated furnishing fabric, blot dyed. The pants
converted from a pair of shorts

124 *Long gown of heavy woollen material, trimming from an old fur coat*

125 *Eighteenth century country girl's costume, made up as follows: Straight wide skirt made from an old sheet, blot dyed and gathered at the waist, over a scoop-necked jumper. Cuffs and fichu made separately from net curtain. Panniers from strip of dyed sheet, gathered at the waist, hitched up and pinned, apron made from sheeting. The bonnet is the bottom of an old frilled petticoat, gathered at the crown*

PLATE 4   *A typical peasant group wearing very simple
costumes of blot dyed old material in earth colours. This
kind of costume takes very little time and only the cost of the
dye (in this aniline dye was used). The sleeves required no
making, as they are old sweaters, the hose are long pants,
dyed, and the shoes are thick socks. These varied earthy
colours sometimes look very beautiful in themselves when
under stage lighting, and form an effective contrast with
more brilliant colours*

126 and 127   Late Victorian music hall costume, based on a polo necked jumper, with addition of frilly false front, the skirt is the underskirt of an evening dress, with a frill made of cheap lining taffeta. The feather boa is authentic, and the hat has been built up with feathers, artificial flowers and a veil, on an old straw shape

Decorated leotards

A simple leotard—nylon or cotton jersey, may form the basis for a quite elaborate costume. The tight skin provides an anchor for disguises of all kinds, and may be worn under any garment as a sure way of holding firmly cloaks or Greek drapery, thus avoiding much fitting and dressmaking.

To use leotards frankly as practice dress with period or characteristic items added, sometimes during the action of a play or dance, is a well known device. It serves well in girls' schools, when the task of making up a believable Victorian gentleman is clearly impossible. Not every play will take this treatment well. It is particularly useful for improvisation, and ad-libbing on a theme, or 'skeleton' dramatic structure, or for plays in which, like *King Lear* the characters are archetypes. It is a good deal less suitable for formal productions of Wilde or Chekov. However, if a play has to be done well in a very short time, it may be a better solution than ill-made, undetailed costumes, and much more creative than hiring.

128 Tabards in dyed hessian and gold painted fabric scraps, with free appliqué and metallic items, worn over jumpers and tights

129 *Plain leotard and tights with masks. These made on wire frames layered with papier mâché, finally painted and decorated. The beards are made from fringing*

130 *The same basic garments with the following added— 'Aztec' masks, made from simple heavy paper shapes, with collage of metallic wrapping papers, and extra trimmings of beads, fringe, rags and feathers. The aprons are fabric scraps with collage decoration, and the jewelry made from fabric, etc (a close up can be seen in illustration 73). This was an intergroup project in a secondary school. The masks were made by second year children, the aprons by third year children and the collars by fourth years. This was part of an art/dance project involving thirty children*

131   The same girls, this time without their tights, wearing
quickly draped pieces of dyed chiffon. The head-dresses are
made from feathers, twigs, beads, etc, and the cornucopia
is illustrated on page 73. When using plastic flowers, we
have found it best to split these and re-assemble them, as
they tend to look rather crude when used whole. It is a pity
to ignore them, as so many are available, but care is needed

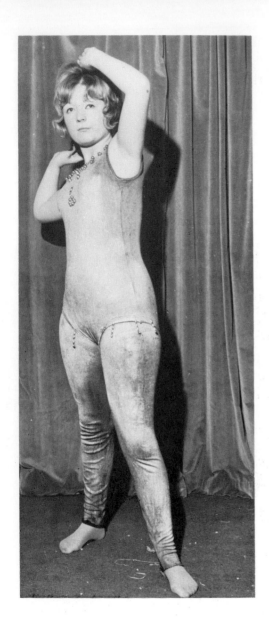

132   Leotard and tights sprayed gold on top of previous gold painting. Spray alone will sink into the fabric and look dull, but it is very useful to add a final sheen. It is best to paint leotards on a model, as they stiffen slightly, and it can be difficult to stretch them into shape

133   Leotard painted with free brush strokes, splashing and spraying. Silver, copper and gold were used on black. This and similar ones, have been used many times as a basis for costumes of fairies, witches and other supernaturals. Be careful when adapting these that back zips are concealed by drapery and decoration. Sleeves are not suitable when dressing this type of character. The mottling produces a blurred effect in movement

134　*Same leotard hung with torn rags in a wide range of dull colours and worn with nylon hair switches, and a wire and paper bird mask*

135   This costume, using a very wide range of torn dyed rags, was based on vest and briefs which had been previously dyed, but a leotard or swimming costume are equally good as foundations. These torn rags give a good effect in movement

136   Angel with torn rag wings, mounted on a halter of gold painted fabric

137 Brilliantly coloured torn rags, mounted on dyed calico
and used with sticks to form wings. When the arms are
lowered, this forms a simple, full garment in one colour, and
the opening and raising of the arms produce a dramatic
effect

105

138 Titania and Bottom from A Midsummer
Night's Dream. *Titania's costume has been
improvised over a decorated leotard*

It is important to remember that the techniques mentioned in this book may be integrated with other work in the field of creative arts and should not be thought of as applicable only to the making of costumes for school plays.

When applied to costume, such techniques as collage, dyeing, printing and embroidery are essentially decorative. The value of the image, where this exceeds decoration, comes when the costume is seen in movement and inter-action with others, in imaginative lighting. The work then certainly transcends in value anything that has been done in the art room. There is much to be said for the view that figurative art, these days, is found at its best on the stage, especially in some of the latest experiments with movement, costumes and lighting.

In the art room, work done for its own sake, while it may use many of the same methods, must stand up by itself. The use of embroidery and fabric printing, and other fabric crafts mainly for decoration, however beautiful, has led to a feeling that these materials are essentially decorative, and cannot be used for more profound purposes. We would like to urge that this is a mistaken idea, and that fabrics and related materials may be used as effectively as paint or stone, by girls and boys for the expression of equally pro-found visual ideas. These materials need not be restricted to a narrow range: stone and fabric, clay and fabric, fabric and heavy junk, and any or all of these combined with lights and mechanical movements are feasible and valuable in art education.

It is our aim to widen the scope of the work, to discourage a narrow craft approach, to avoid the sex-typing of work in art departments, and to bring about creative thinking.

Further reading

OUTLINE OF ENGLISH COSTUMES *Doreen Yarwood* Batsford,
London: Plays Inc, Boston
ARMOUR AND WEAPONS *Paul Martin* Herbert Jenkins, London
DESIGNING AND MAKING STAGE COSTUME *Motley* Studio Vista,
London
EVOLUTION OF FASHION *Margot Hamilton-Hill and P. Bucknell*
Batsford, London: Reinhold, New York
COSTUME CAVALCADE *Henry Harold Hanson* Methuen, London
INTRODUCING JEWELRY MAKING *John Crawford* Batsford,
London: Watson-Guptill, New York
A HISTORY OF COSTUMES IN THE WEST *F. Bouchers* Thames and
Hudson, London
MEDIEVAL THEATRE COSTUME *Iris Brooke* Black, London
COSTUME IN THE ANCIENT WORLD *James Laver* Faber, London
INTRODUCING MACHINE EMBROIDERY *Ira Lillow* Batsford,
London: Watson-Guptill, New York
TEXTILE PRINTING AND DYEING *Nora Proud* Batsford, London:
Reinhold, New York
INTRODUCING TEXTILE PRINTING *Nora Proud* Batsford, London:
Watson-Guptill, New York
DESIGNING WITH STRING *Mary Seyd* Batsford, London:
Watson-Guptill, New York
INTRODUCING BATIK *Evelyn Samuel* Batsford, London:
Watson-Guptill, New York
CREATIVE TEXTILE CRAFT: THREAD AND FABRIC *Rolf Hartung*
Batsford, London: Van Nostrand Reinhold, New York
COLOUR AND TEXTURE IN CREATIVE TEXTILE CRAFT *Rolf Hartung*
Batsford, London: Van Nostrand, Reinhold, New York
CREATIVE PAPERCRAFT *Ernst Röttger* Batsford, London: Van
Nostrand Reinhold, New York
COSTUME IN DETAIL *Nancy Bradfield* Harrap, London: Plays
Inc, Boston
THE HISTORY OF COSTUME *Margaret Stavridi* Hugh Evelyn,
London: Plays Inc, Boston
THEATRICAL COSTUME AND THE AMATEUR STAGE *Michael Green*
Arco, London: Plays Inc, Boston
MEDIEVAL AND TUDOR COSTUME *Phillis Cunnington* Faber,
London: Plays Inc, Boston

Suppliers

Helizarin dye and Binder D

Skilbeck Brothers Limited
Bagnall House, 55–7 Glengall Road, London SE15

Printex (Tinolite) and Binder CM

Winsor and Newton
Education Division, Wealdstone, Harrow, Middlesex

Geigy (UK) Limited 42 Berkeley Square, London W1
and Simonsway, Manchester 22

Dylon and Procion dyes

Mayborne Products Limited
139–47 Sydenham Road, London SE26

Metallic powder and aniline dyes

Brodie and Middleton
74 Long Acre, London WC2

Marvin Medium and school art supplies

Margros Limited
Monument House Monument Way West,
Woking, Surrey

Cheap fabrics and remnants

Bradley Textiles Ltd
15 Stott Street, Nelson, Lancashire

Cheap bulk fabrics and dressmakers' sundries

McCullock and Wallis
Dering Street, London W1

Beads, stage jewels, etc.

Fred Aldous Ltd
Manchester
and The Bead Shop
South Molton Street, London W1

Paraffin wax

The Hygenol Company Ltd
Rothwell-Haigh, Leeds, Yorks.

USA

Acco-Lite

American Crayon Company
Sandusky, Ohio

Alizarin

American Cyanamid Company, Dyer Division
Princetown, New Jersey

Procion dye stuffs

Chemical Manufacturing Company
Madison Avenue, New York, NY

ICI Organics Inc.
55 Canal Street, Providence, Rhode Island, NY 02901

Versatex

Durable Arts
Box 2413, San Rafael, California 94901

Marvin Medium

Eagle Pencil Company
Danbury, Connecticut

Beads, sequins

Hollander Bead and Novelty Corporation
25 West 37 Street, New York 18, NY

Amor Bead and Pearl Company Inc.
19001 Stringway, Long Island City, NY